Shouting at the Moon

Poems by
Jimmy Rodda

'All poetry is magic. It is a spell against insensitivity, failure of imagination, ignorance and barbarism.'

Charles Causley

For Stephen

Acknowledgements

Cover Design by Charlotte Cooper

Acknowledgements are due to the editors of the following publications in which some of these poems first appeared: *Ambit, Carillon, Cake, Dream Catcher, Orbis, South, The Cannon's Mouth, The Frogmore Papers, The Journal.*

Contents

The Bishop

I stared out through the stained glass window
                    and heard the bishop sigh
raindrops were bouncing off chicken wire
                    you must take control of
                    your life and get off the
I turned and screw-eyed his chasuble
he was out of his leather armchair
                    god cares for the oppressed
                    every living creature
I stumbled held out my clumsy hand

he was recoiled and standing off me
                    rely on sentiment
                    and people will tire of
I dragged back something from my childhood
about Jesus and the prostitute
                    have this card and here`s a
                    coin the world is heartless
and I left him to his library

the water poured down my face and neck
                    my son we are one world
god I shouted for christsake help me
save me from this fucking state of mind
                    alcohol opium
                    drugs to be wary of
                    important to phone the
                    centre such good people
I launched a foot towards the gate and
the door closed quietly behind me

Black on Maroon

(For Rothko)

what I see
are standing stone structures
rough-edged
a poisonous coagulating smog
taking temporary shape

it`s a window
black oil on maroon
a whisper
to the frailty of
concrete and glass

was it John

                           was it John Updike who said

that those who suffer from psoriasis

              see the world beneath the skin

                       Dennis Potter was another

whose awareness of the BULLSHIT that is swallowed

                  dug us deep below the surface

is it then my crabby flaking

          itching skin that I should blame

                    for the YEARS

spent struggling upstream

      PERHAPS

    just don`t expect sympathy for the surface tension

the cosmetics

      YOU

                 who`ve had it easy

hide behind

Manhattan Made

this little volume attracted me
pitted and dog-eared from New York nineteen thirty
syncretism in a kind of confused key
who were you Charles Recht

pitted and dog-eared from New York nineteen thirty
orange-bound scribbled in with coarse paper and dirty
who were you Charles Recht
with Marauding in May and A Man on the Ferry

orange-bound scribbled in with coarse paper and dirty
Eliot-drenched you offered A Modern Litany
with Marauding in May and A Man on the ferry
who were you

Eliot-drenched you offered A Modern Litany
with something called the Aria Parlante
who were you
on air in April nineteen thirty

with something called the Aria Parlante
syncretism in a kind of confused key
on air in April nineteen thirty
this little volume attracted me

Three Studies

(From Bacon`s Figures at the Base of a Crucifixion)

we are a bare-backed hunched
excuse for an eagle
weak limbs dead winged
head carried low
eyesight hampered by violent hair
less god in his image more earthenware

we are a blinded breathless chicken
fat and ready for plucking
straining our scrawny neck
teeth gritted and artless
lost white-bandaged sucking air
perched one-legged broken bare

we are a bloodied screeching hyena
white mouthed lean ribbed
muscle and sinew twisted
in defence of the last kill

in creature comfort in country air
we have a culture but not there

BIG ISSUE

I watched him from the other side
as he stood selling his paper
one Sunday morning by Poundland

he`d been around had several day`s growth
was wearing John Lennon glasses
a black trenchcoat and was chewing gum

he had a line of sympathy
from well-dressed older ladies
three stopped at different times to talk

a bitter breeze blew down the street
I thrust my hands inside my jeans
and stamped my feet and spat and coughed

the red bandana set it off
an attempt to look interesting
I thought so I walked across to see

why the poppy in February
I said and then wished I hadn`t
as he looked at me well gone

there was something lost and wounded
in his eyes then he tried to speak
but what came out was dry and choked

While men are gazing up to Heaven
Imagining after a happiness
he paused searching my expression

Or fearing a Hell after they are dead
blue eyes that once were beautiful
begged me bloodied for agreement

Their eyes are put out
That they see not what is their birthrights
I moved but could not shake his gaze

the local vicar rescued me
striding down towards his matins
I thought that I`d enlist his help

here mate I said give one to me
held it out and cried BigIssue
bless you said man of god and brushed on past

RELIGION

Religion, narcotic extract derived from
the immature fruits of human consciousness,
native to the species homo sapiens.
The sugary, superstitious substance
is normally refined to an orthodox powder
with a sharp, bitter taste.

Drugs derived from religion include
Christianity, *Judaism*, *Sikhism*
and *Islam*. Because these drugs can cause
severe physical and psychological dependence,
they are used as a form of social control
by some governments.

The period necessary for dependency to occur varies with
the type of religion and the amount and frequency of dose.
With religions of the evangelical and fundamentalist type,
harm is expressed through a propensity for
trance-like states, prostration, intellectual sterility
and abrogation of personal responsibility.

These effects may lead to disruption of
personal and family relationships, economic loss and,
in some circumstances, begging on the streets. When
religion-use is stopped, withdrawal symptoms may occur,
the discomfort, intensity and duration varying with
the type of religion, sect or cult, and degree of dependence.

Withdrawal symptoms include alterations in behaviour, excitation of the nervous system and initial feelings of depression and anxiety. However, the most severe symptoms normally disappear within ten days, leaving the individual with greater confidence, self-respect and a sharper sense that other people matter too.

Unquiet Mind

Friends to the death, bottles of vodka and martini,
on the balcony where you stumbled and smoked butt-ends,
railing against *the shit uncertainty of it all*,

Brian, you barely existed then. With plans to meet
Roman Polanski pissed away one mad afternoon,
it was a jabbering, manic, relentless decline,
and what did they do to help you? Sent the fire brigade,
not once but twice, while somehow you kept alive the self-

delusion of sanity. *Collect two hundred pounds*
as you pass Go, a collection of cuttings, vinyl LPs,
various poems, some that rhymed, and numbered tee-shirts.
If only life were monopoly money, old boy,
successful journalist, author. Fallen on hard times.

Lovely girl

Jehovah made an appearance today,
easy August morning, while I drank tea.
He resembled three ladies of sixty
or so, on doorstop duty with a bloke,
very *middle aged*, brief-cased, in charge. And
a lovely young girl about seventeen.
Her hair was long and tied back. Simple dress.

JEHOVAH APPEARED IN ST. JUST AT TEN,
EARLY ENOUGH TO TALK, OR TO LISTEN.

She met me with a smile and employed the
usual strategy. You know, we`re all
sinners, then she blushed. Plain, beautiful girl.

Who will speak for her, be worldly when the
hate is thrown about clothes, ideas, boys.
Yahweh? For God`s sake do not make me laugh.

YOU, THE FUTURE

Tonight we drink our wine and lager, the
mood that fuels us, Afghanistan; you point
to Rothko`s towering vision and laugh, is
truth confined to television, evil to
a single man? You drag in smoke, you change
position, find a bottle, uncork it.

Tonight we drink and talk about a point
of light that is Rigel, and really is
there *nothing to be done*. You ask me to
believe there was a prophet who could change
the world if only others would allow it.
The fire and wine are red and comforting, the

night outside the window. We drink. And is
the Tate St. Ives a little shoddy to
be honest something cheap that needs to change
about the stairs and then what`s in it
yes there`s Heron and Alfred Wallis the
real poet now that is art there is the point.

Tonight we drink. We talk and laugh and drink to
Benn but not to Thatcher little bastard change
means worse in that case and Costello summed it
up in something called *dance on your grave* the
lovely bloke he`s a grown man he said the point
is where`s compassion that is

due to you and me the wine is lovely change
it fruity sparkle deep and red it
isn`t bad for two pound fifty raise the
glass like the titanic grasp the point
of the nettle of the leader where is
love lionel when you most need it to

begin to obliviate and then it
is that we come full circle when the
conversation dies until a final point
of rage that the sad truth of the matter is
that *eventually* you realise too
that luca brasi sleeps with the losers change

it the point is bomb the people for democracy
£5 gift voucher for freedom change it
to you have seen the movie this is real

Freefall

I've danced with joy up a pathway
towards a room of loud music and bodies
where sweet excitement, love, tore down the night.
I've seen a man's dignity gorged by triumph,
consumed with evangelical blood-lust,
abasement before power.
I've understood the function of propaganda.
I've known the thrill of fatherhood,
been absent while others slipped away.
My past crawls all over me.
It shivers, grey voices chatter in my head.
God bless she said.
I live in a bearable climate,
work to pay my way,
have company,
drink beer and wine by the sea.
And I'm a cornered rodent,
scrabbling on a splintered incline,
spitting at the hand that feeds me,
trapped,
but less gullible, maybe.

I am told to value freedom.
Was I, ever, free?

When I look into the glass

When I look into the glass it`s plain to see
the shadows creeping closer and, you know,
there is no God, there`s only you and me.

We learn the lesson young, with certainty,
that pain will hurt and sometimes life is slow.
When I look into the glass it`s plain to see.

Would *goodness* sanction Nature`s cruelty?
Conscious creatures know they have to go.
There is no God, there`s only you and me.

The ancients thought of life as mystery,
invented spirit, learnt to scrape and bow.
When I look into the glass it`s plain to see.

Know how to love, that`s where we find the key
to better Nature, rise above the clay. Know
there is no God, there`s only you and me.

You try to be the best that you can be,
face up to truth, refuse to let your head hang low.
When I look into the glass it`s plain to see
there is no God, there`s only you and me.

Another Spring

Water burned our tongues and throats,
stunted living children`s growth,
we spluttered out our lungs, our eyes,
darkness screamed, we were crucified.

In time, Allah, we will survive,
when Truth is no longer paralysed;
sick of shit and apple pie,
we`ll sing the Devil`s lullaby.

And who`ll guard your guards from Holy Slaughter
when we cleanse our souls in sewage water?

So laugh and sing, join wringing choirs,
we shall build an Easter fire.

Loss

I have a present for you she
said and gave me a pebble and
a little slate picked off a beach
I said I would treasure them and
I did they are on my desk now

she would have misery moments
when a tear would sparkle in the
corner of an eye and there was
so much there below that needed
healing and her colour sense was
so remarkable I loved her
accent and the cry of the gulls

the wine made you laugh and I saw
you begin to enjoy who you
are and you shook your head at the
shorts that I wore under my jeans
and you were puzzled at the look
in my eyes and asked what is it

the bottle is a difficult
object to ignore and this one
sparkled too and it has to be
said is so sourly seductive
at times but is a lesser truth
stop all the clocks they say. Love is dead.

ON THE EDGE

This has put me on edge,
this SITUATION.
Tonight I am close to the phone.

You wanted me to keep my word and I have.
If you want,
we can destroy the evidence together.

Sure,
if you want,
suicide is an important way to die.

But I have survived this and I kept my word
and I am here,
rambling like some rusty Bible,
waiting by the phone.
I kept my word.
Truth and lies keep us alive.

why

(i.m. Anne Sexton)

why did I want to kill nana
how else could I feel powerful
a nothing crouching in the closet
being sick and I mean living sick
I read fairy tales

I didn`t know she was suffering
I wouldn`t have gone with the boys
which was awful and powerful
and like a nightmare it kept being true
but she got sick and wanted to be
my mother`s child

and she led a very full life
and I am powerful
and I am nana in order to kill her
the nana I didn`t want
she died and I was pregnant with joy

SUNDIAL

Cracked and faded from my purple
I feel lost, confused
Sad remnant of a better time

Tutankhamon treasured me
And now I exist
Here
Damaged but alive
Breathing…just
As old as the sand

Time teller
Or was
I live in the nether world
A lopsided tombstone

How I wish for life
My master`s imperial, pretty head
But the golden child has turned to dust
The world decays
And the sun is dead

Screaming Paul

Birdman,
dyed ginger hair,
ear-ringed, glasses,
perched on the roof.
Waiting.

Hiding
in your tent in the living room,
drink and drugs,
rowdy music,
cracked window,
scattered shoes.
A grown man using wet wipes.

There was of course a public execution,
neighbours like bees at a honeycomb,
streetlights burning brown,
vomit green with blood.
Drowning.

You grew in the shadow of Wesley`s tree;
Paul, you are now as free as you can be.

Curious Logic

Whisper to me near the toxic flame,
speak sweetly to me, tell yourself the lie,
breathe curious logic, face it just the same.

Chatter to me, give yourself a name,
spin out your truth, preach to me, clarify;
whisper to me near the toxic flame.

Pass on your wisdom, put me in the frame,
appease the flock with hope they won`t deny,
breathe curious logic, face it just the same.

Parade your intellectual acclaim,
pray fantasies to those who will comply,
whisper to me near the toxic flame.

Articulate the cliché without shame,
soliloquize, act loud and magnify;
breathe curious logic, face it just the same.

Submit, prostrate yourself and play the game,
renounce your sins, then look me in the eye;
whisper to me near the toxic flame,
breathe curious logic, face it just the same.

He made concrete paving slabs

As the months ploughed on
and searching for his strength,
he watched as they took shape,
concealing the dirt and pebble-strewn floor
of our back yard and the useless drain.

Concrete cancer, broken, decayed;
gone.

Elmer

(Fond memories)

When you browbeat the other
second-hand salesmen into
collecting for the Salvation Army.
When you made friends with Jim Lefferts,
enlisted his help,
drank his whisky.

When you gained the attention of Sister Shara
and distracted her from
the old time religion.
When you preached hell-fire and damnation,
pulled off the baseball slide,
glared wild-eyed.

When you showed compassion for Lulu Baines
after she sideswiped you,
the oldest badger game in the book.
When you grew to self-knowledge
and shook your head at
the attempted miracle.

Then,
when you survived the fire,
became a man
and put aside childish things.
"St. Paul. First Corinthians. 13:11"
Now that WAS inspired.

Mother

The words are there inside my head,
fond memories of what was said,
singing to me.
You and me will be
the greatest pardners,
buddies and pals.

Winding through Cornish lanes
this winter night,
under a cold sky,
grey turning to black;
the words are there for miles,
singing to me.
Oh the moon shines bright
for Charlie Chaplin,
his boots are cracklin.

Returning home tonight,
remembering the camphorated oil
and other words,
not singing,
whispered,
breathing, hanging by a thread;
God bless, she said.

Bing

(For Tony Crosby)

Sitting, playing stupid games, half listening,
peering outside the door at greener fields;
Mr. Crosby, legs crossed, reading Milton,
Duckworth mouthing daft comments, unconcealed.
Then the salvation of the fire alarm,
bad boys on the yard and the register.

But there was also Cade by James Hadley Chase
and your comment that I wrote about it
with enthusiasm "in the spirit
of the entertainment industry".
How would I assess it as Literature?
Pennies, you might say, began to drop.

I left the place at sixteen, too early,
wanting the pub and the sweet power of sin.
Tony, best teacher, you gave me Beckett,
and let me see "the skull beneath the skin".

Lucifer

A brief place to rest my head;
my friend, a moment in the shadows,
a pause for breath, in my flight,
in my struggle for a justice.

He has pursued me since almost
the beginning, across the ages,
and is getting close again.

I spoke for something better
not perfect, but an understanding
of our base reality,
of the urge to make a justice
in a ruthless universe.

His response? Jealous, petty,
unjust, vindictive, bloodthirsty;
and with all the arrogant swagger
of the malevolent bully that he is.

His method? How much do you want?
Child sacrifice, disembowelment
for those who disagreed with him,
torture by stoning, death by fire.
His murderous angels instigating
a "Holy" Civil War,
the agonized death of millions of innocents,
the Flood, and more!
It`s all there in the book,
if you care to look,
and he calls ME a terrorist.

29

A brief place to rest my head;
my friend, a moment in the shadows,
a pause for breath, in my flight,
in my struggle for a justice.

Istanbul

We drive through a huge, clean city
abundant with flowers as we pass by
on our way to the old quarter,
a small hotel, balcony, a view.

We walk on Saturday night at ten.
Families have their picnics,
fruit drinks and blankets spread out on the grass.

We sit on a bench, inside our thoughts,
charmed by this wise old lady,
at peace with herself and the sea.
Tomorrow we return home.

Another Day

The wall clock chimed at ten past five,
one hour before a drink today;
I read the book to sixty four
and saw Lorraine, had things to say.

Outside Adele, at ninety two,
shuffled on and picked her way
along the street against the breeze,
a weary heart, another day.

Storms in Portreath and broken walls,
and boats were sunk and work delayed;
men looking lost standing around,
no chance to go to sea, get paid.

And here I sit and watch the rain,
the chopping sea across the bay,
the broken fence and hanging tree,
the debris of another day.

Lenin

There was a knock on the door this morning.
It was Lenin. I`d seen him look better.
He had a battered rucksack on his back
and wanted a cup of tea and some bread.
He`d pay for it, he said. I wasn`t sure
but invited him in, boiled the kettle.

"They`ve pulled down another statue," he said.
"Yes I saw it in the evening paper."
"Bastards," he said, "For god`s sake don`t they think?"
"Religious terminology," I said.
"*Metaphysics*. It just won`t go away.
Perhaps sometime…maybe…another day!"

The way he looked I thought that he`d explode;
I filled his flask and sent him down the road.

Good News

The weather was fine, it was June or July.
We found a place to park. The room was buzzing
and the appointment late by two hours.

Not everyone was receiving good news.
That much was clear. I read the leaflets.
Men can get it too, that kind of cancer.

Then they were ready. We took a deep breath
and made our way through. He removed your bandage.
"Go open the champagne." Outside the sunshine
mingled with petrol fumes and rush hour traffic.

You looked at me and, at last, the mask slipped.

The Last One

(In memory of Primo Levi)

We returned from our work between the
black sky and the mud of the road
but did not, tonight, break out of the column.
Instead we marched on to the roll-call square,
the glaring searchlight and the gallows that were there.

The band played something raucous, hollow;
then the drill of *Mutzen ab*, hats off.
The space took time to fill, crunching shoes on dirty snow.
Silence was ordered, angrily,
and the condemned man was hauled before us.

What had he done, steal bread, try to escape?
The speech went on and then: *"Habt ihr verstanden"?*
We, all of us, mumbled *"Jawohl"*,
standing there, knowing it was the last days,
and still an example must be made.

Then a naked cry rang above all our heads:
"Comrades, I am the last one!"
But we stayed still, all of us, eyes lowered,
and the trapdoor dropped and the band played again
and we filed past the body of the dying man.

For Me

For me it was falling from a bike
onto gravel in the corner of the rec,
grazing my elbows on both arms.
Shortly after I found
psoriasis where I had bled.
My aunty had it, yes,
and I know it is supposed to be
hereditary but I did wonder.

For me it is the itch that hurts
and the snow-flake cascading, ruined
deformity of a tender scalp;
unclean, dandruffed but a lifetime worse
and more. I wear white and dappled grey
to hide the falling scabs, the sin.
So, young, I learned to scratch and bleed,
and grew to know the fire beneath my skin.

Jumping Shafts

We have been to the valley;
as children too, not knowing the danger
a failed leap or lunge could bring.

Running through gorse and bramble,
jumping shafts at Grenville Mine
like condemned men
running for the taste of freedom.
We grew on adrenalin,
the restless thrill of those blue-grey days.

We have been to the valley, briefly,
walking home on dark and quiet roads
to squash and saffron cake for tea.

Limping Through

I limp among the debris of summer,
those blazing hot, high, breathless days.
Furkan`s abandoned fire engine,
Jasmine`s weather vane, stuck in a patch of earth,
the go-kart, wheel-buckled, dented, scuffed,
all lie on the dry, burnt grass.

I limp through this tired, late August day
and the chill east breeze cuts through me.
The sun shines on but is weak and cracked,
and, as I pause on the broken seat,
the hours are speeding faster by.
Autumn days are moving closer now.

Alleys

(For Geoff)

You told me this, Geoff,
about a marble you had as a boy,
an alley.
It was green and cloudy and chipped,
but with a gleam all of its own,
saturated with sunlight, you said,
treasured above all the rest.

You loved the unsmooth feel of it
under the tip of your finger,
and it seemed as hard to you
as the granite underneath our feet.
It was unique.

Grandad gave it to you,
broken off the neck of
an empty lemonade bottle.
"There you are my `andsome.
That`ll win you plenty more".

But you lost it
playing with the bigger boys,
surrendered it inside a half circle
drawn by a ragged stick.
And it was gone;
its contours,
the curving grooved wave across the surface,
every beloved blemish, pocketed and gone.

Afterwards Grandad handed you a fistful,
half a dozen more lemonade alleys
catching the light in his hand.
It was a lesson you should have learned early
you said, mysteriously.

The Old Rugged Cross
was sung softly today;
a quiet hymn for a gentle life.

Moby

The fog came down this week
on the Roseland, hanging there,
and the rain, Cornish rain
dripping on sodden fields
day after day
and, drop by drop, the resolve ebbed away.

There is blood in the water
and you know what I should do;
but the great sperm whale hangs in the balance
and I`m no longer sure.
Call me Ishmael or call me stupid,
it won`t wash.

Black Hour

I am not to blame for the shadows
that crowd in on me in the black hour
shapes that rise and fall and dance and die
that live on the wall of this curtained cell
and the dark that hurts as sure as hell

and you can we talk can we *communicate*
you picked up the page can you relate
to this can words survive the chaos
between us can they stumble out to
meet you in the turmoil of this night

are you of this or another time
am I a job to do which grey faces
peer across *your* shoulder dare you feel the
texture of the fear how did you lose your
freedom *my dear* for once we both were free

Battery Hen

She is useful to us,
giving us our daily eggs
from her industrial, beak-trimmed,
force moulted world,
scrabbling, as she does, on her low lit
sloping floor, unaware of sunshine,
captive witness to our cold efficiency.

With dim, uncomprehending eyes
she stares back
but cannot talk to us,
living blind,
artless, innocent,
pecking at the wire, as she must,
being what she is.

We find her useful,
enjoying our daily eggs,
innocent, artless,
living blind.

Goodbye Carrick Roads

It lies deep on the Fal estuary,
wide and proud on a wet and windy coast,
this drowned, meandering river valley,
Karrek Reun, childhood memory, the most
natural of harbours flowing to the sea.
Carrick Roads, created by the Ice Age,
you have spent a lifetime cradling me;
I drink the view and fear and worry fades.
Yet as I shield my eyes at the gateway,
like some time lord stiff at his terminal
and watch the flocks of wintering sea birds sway,
this place seems, like me, ephemeral.
I`ll take the ferry to Seal Rock, maybe
a fond goodbye, a final odyssey.

For and after John Clare

You felt you were, you only knew you were,
you said, a plodding shadow, "dull and void",
chilled in spirit, earthly pain incurred,
battered, life and liberty destroyed.
Uncommon poet, vernacular and real,
your living lines of speech, earthy, intense;
your vivid diction altered how we feel,
that`s all, and from a rustic, native innocence.
But lesser talents drove you to despair,
they could not know and did not understand;
the literati drank a different air
from the common man who worked upon the land.
Unshackled soul, you needed to be free,
and troubled, human, you will do for me.

Old Stones

We were born in a land built upon old stones,
the last of an ancient race,
survivors of a peninsular kingdom,
hardened, buoyed up by the granite beneath our feet.

We walked among citadels of weathered moorstone,
streams and wells, rocking logan boulders;
we played by Carwynnen Quoit and among the menhir,
standing stone circles on Bodmin Moor.

We were fed by copper and tin and fish and china clay;
and though even rocks decay
and one day our day is done,
we lived our lives, we danced in the sun.

Thin Times

These are thin times. Rosie, struggling at 91,
Ross at 92, fallen, hospital bound;
mud is choking the guttering
and summer is a comin in
like the stench of rotten seaweed.

The fir tree`s branches were ripped off
after you replanted the flowers the cats tore up,
and that dismembered pheasant on the road
was writhing in agony but I drove on while you
stuffed peelings and mouldy bread in plastic sacks.

I am keeping out of it, giving nothing away,
while you play lip service to mediocrity,
the latest singing sensation and X Factor,
and the local painters waiting for their Godot.
I must remember not to sing.

The light that shone for us

We were not, perhaps, what we took ourselves to be,
were never clinging, close, as some would understand
but we more than shared a lifetime`s energy
and we fed each other, didn`t we, you and me?

Now you wait with crumbling cake and awkward hands,
the mind plays tricks and steals identity;
the day ends quietly, as it began,
and gloomy shadows creep across the land.

But as we wait, and with the darkness comes the dust,
I still recall the blinding light that shone for us.

Still in hope (and only ten lines)

Here I am, tight-fisted and feverish,
lifting a glass of the old *Famous Grouse*
to the toast of our revolutionaries.
And to you, like a ravenous pilgrim,
I come with my pure bleeding heart bearing
gifts of my blood, lost liver, and my songs.
Yet all the plans lie still-born and tangled,
and still I involve myself with failure,
schemes and dreams, and the hopes of the hopeless,
sweet secular prayers that life has mangled.

Getting by

A rough night and fallen tree,
hanging cables and power lines
have hindered our normal routine.
Darkness sits in the corner,
allowing in the night; we are
more pensive than we might have been.

Carousing in candle light,
inspecting red wine through crystal glass,
held up to the hearth and the flames.
An evening of double speak,
the room shrunken to what we can see;
every thing something we might reclaim.

You speak up for longevity;
you want to outlive the TV
like others who saw the back of steam trains.
I recall Bruce and the spider and say:
"You know you might if you try hard enough."
(Not for me to say something inane).

But I understand, I really do.
It is to know you had a purpose;
that's it, your life had meaning too.

Summers Beach in Winter

The beach belongs to me right now
and the chill December breeze that
blows across the empty bay.
The small stone steps are perilous.

I tread a very careful way
past the Harbour Master`s hut
and the battered concrete slipway
to the pebbles, sand and safety.

I know this place from memory.
The waters where we swam and sailed,
and rockpools where the children played,
seem smaller now, a fairytale.

As I make my way across the weed
and the shrieking gulls that block my way,
there's an early moon in the white and grey.
After, breathless, I face the sea
and raise my collar to the waves:
Just you and me and yesterday.

Where We Belong

(i.m. Joaquim Cardozo)

In the cemetery of childhood
where the flowers are in bloom,
with the pains of adolescence
and where hope lies in the womb.

In the sweetness of the morning,
with the pangs of motherhood,
with the ashes of the homeless,
the sick, misunderstood.

In the footsteps of Winstanley,
with the legions of the poor,
with those who suffer mental anguish,
where the hungry cry for more.

In the shoes of the Mahatma,
where most normal folk align,
in the grim, oppressive sweatshops,
where the put upon combine.

At the feet of Albert Einstein,
the persecution of the gay,
with the godlike and the godless,
with the addict gone astray.

With the migrants by the roadside,
with the prisoner on Death Row
where the tattered wings of angels
need a love we need to know.

Purple Lilac

He was tidying the outhouse,
a perennial but neglected job,
when he found her old scrapbook
in the corner of a broken cabinet.
He called for me to have a look,
handling it reverently
like a treasure that might disintegrate.
We blew the dust and picked away cobwebs,
and took it outside to a picnic table,
which had itself seen better days.

Inside the first page was a pressed flower,
a Purple Lilac, bright, pristine.
He smoothed its petals,
as her fingers would have done,
squeezed the stem, blew again and smiled:
"Who would want to be a woman?"
A breeze played through the hedgerow
and I walked away inside.
When I thought I heard him speak to it,
I caught my breath, stood quietly aside.

Blank is Beautiful

It is a small window but lets in the light,
depatterning souls can be such a delight.
You see that we care for you, welcome your trust,
electroshock therapy and angel dust.
High voltage to genitals is a real scream,
it changes opinions, kills self-esteem.
It`s especially interesting when you convulse,
and the foetal curled coma, the loss of your pulse.
Dismantling your person is what we`re about,
we adhere to our mission, call us devout.
We like the blank slate, to erase who you were,
tabula rasa is the state we prefer.
Oh yes, you can cry for your mother, Ariz,
and you have always loved us. We aim to please.

Dearly Departed

Comforting, in the end, the door closes
respectfully, we sit with my brothers
and their wives, and the Bentley moves off at
a funereal pace, well then what else,

as if egg shells would be broken but they
were smashed some time ago, dear departed.
Expensive, this affair, and expected.
And there is snow, damping the wiper blades

that gravely mark time like a metronome,
dragging us into the day, the moment.
One of the wives mouths an inanity
about feeling guilty at times like this.

I have sunk to the level of the split
infinitive, obviously, but where
is or was the love, from the old man
down to me?

Maybe tonight is for understanding,
not now, with what is left of these people.
Dearly departed indeed but, truly,
there was nothing that was cheap about *him*.

Endgame? Newquay?

Where the raging Atlantic meets Fistral Beach
and surfers ride the wind to find a wave,
I sip green tea in the Headland Hotel
while flying rats dip and squawk and sway outside
and steal from everything that moves.
The place is full of strangers.
No real people live here do they, no locals?
I am here from choice and won`t take a room.

When I can I pull myself up to take the air.
The stumble goes unnoticed, I think,
but the shake is mostly who I am.
It helps to think of Stephen now at times like this,
a braver man than I am Gunga Din!
It could be worse. On the other hand
why make the journey to Beachy Head,
when you can drop from The Island instead.

Almost Blue

The wheels on the bus go round and round,
and the streets of St. Day are where they always were.
The seats have surely bruised the backside,
neither they or it built for comfort or for speed.

Every bump and pothole issues a strong reminder
that this sluggish muscular disorder shall not be forgotten.
Then, up ahead, from a tired and dirty sky,
two shafts of light spear through the grey;

and there it is, the crack, *it's how the light gets in.*
Perhaps they are here to rescue the rest of the day.
Short lived but welcome, this relieves
the mood of the moment which was, for me, almost blue.

This condition must look choreographed,
the shake an integral part of the routine, so that like a
newborn needing to stand its ground the bell is found and
pushed, the machine shudders to a stop.

This place is a brushstroke in time, walls and houses
painted in black and white, stark reminder
of a granite childhood, an attitude;
there is more to do than just live with it.

Evensong

Evensong. St. Just Church.
Standing in the damp and the chill
above the churchyard, breathing dead thoughts,
the day still, as spent as an archaic ritual.
He lies among the flowers
and there will be no raising of the shroud,
no refurbishment with fresh blood
pumping through the veins,
no rolling away the stone.
Only scars, faded from their purple,
scorched earth blasted by a searing sun
and then the dust.

Vanity Mirror

Looking closely at what is left
Wiping away the mist
Peering deeper at the bristly psoriatic face
Eyes that are still blind
Dark eyed pupils round and deaf
Shop-soiled grin through the atoms and decay
The face of the electric chair
Catch your breath and laugh boy
Sucking the tongue through gritted teeth
Mouth agape staring into nothing
A black orifice
Blacker than any blindness

Lockdown

clouds run in a warm sky
without a shift in gears
drawing us into daylight
pure enough to drink
attic windows catch the sun
on the roof where seagulls
take their daily walk
blossom blooms again
in this shelter from the hurricane
now we must dream our dreams
in a narrow space of life
how stupidly we steer this course
what do the clocks say
time is in my pocket
for now I am in the sun
growing deaf
beaten by the breeze
breathless

Standing on the edge

Why not come and stand with me?
Be a friend. As the sky dims towards Autumn
we can perch on the edge of an evening chill
above the sandstone drop at Ganow Yfarn.
Let`s take the pathway
that winds down beyond our sight,
risking the gulls and a rockfall,
stepping towards the sea
over broken slate and gorse and bramble.

We can find our cave down there
over the rocks, scrape our knees,
sing our rhymes and clap our hands.
We can sit cross-legged and listen to
the music as waves wash up
over stones and gravel;
we can wash the salt from our lips.
It will be enough won`t it
as the evening draws in?

Shouting at the Moon

"I tried my best. I did."
With hands cupped and breathing visible,
shouting at the moon,
the old bike spluttering for some sort of life,
breaking the other silence.

The call of a fox, or perhaps the beast,
somewhere far off, high on Rough Tor.
Then, shouting at the moon again:
"I tried my best to understand!"

A strange, creeping cold on Bodmin Moor,
burnt black sky and me,
shouting at the moon,
lifting my head like a wolf.

"Tell whoever it concerns.
I tried my best. I did!"

Copyright 2024 Jimmy Rodda

ISBN: 9798878525848

Printed in Great Britain
by Amazon

38334593R00046